JUN 1 9 2017

3 1994 01556 6729

SANTA ANA PUBLIC LIBRARY

D0770945

J SP 575.54 BIS
Bishop, Celeste
Por que las plantas
  tienen raices?

                          $23.60
CENTRAL   31994015566729

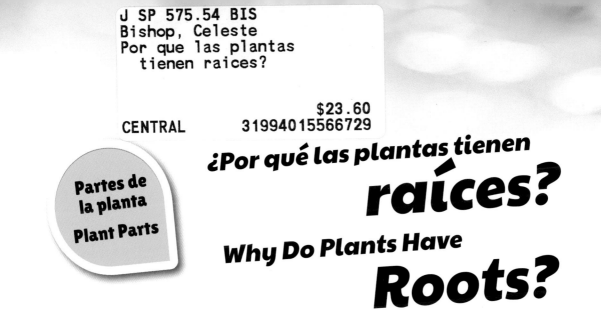

Partes de
la planta
Plant Parts

¿Por qué las plantas tienen raíces?

Why Do Plants Have Roots?

Celeste Bishop

Traducido por Eida de la Vega

PowerKiDS
press.

New York

Published in 2016 by The Rosen Publishing Group, Inc.
29 East 21st Street, New York, NY 10010

Copyright © 2016 by The Rosen Publishing Group, Inc.

All rights reserved. No part of this book may be reproduced in any form without permission in writing from the publisher, except by a reviewer.

First Edition

Editor: Sarah Machajewski
Book Design: Mickey Harmon
Translator: Eida de la Vega

Photo Credits: Cover, p. 6 (plant) Filipe B. Varela/Shutterstock.com; cover (sky) Elenamiv/Shutterstock.com; cover, p. 1 (logo, frame) Perfect Vectors/Shutterstock.com; cover, pp. 1, 3–4, 7–8, 11–12, 15–16, 19–20, 23–24 (background) djgis/Shutterstock.com; p. 5 Richard Griffin/Shutterstock.com; p. 9 Brian A Jackson/Shutterstock.com; p. 10 LilKar/Shutterstock.com; p. 13 Gyuszko-Photo/Shutterstock.com; p. 14 Yuji Sakai/Photodisc/Getty Images; pp. 17, 18 showcake/Shutterstock.com; p. 21 Sergiy Bykhunenko/Shutterstock.com; p. 22 Julie Campbell/Shutterstock.com

Cataloging-in-Publication Data

Bishop, Celeste, author.
 Why do plants have roots? = ¿Por qué las plantas tienen raíces? / Celeste Bishop.
    pages cm. — (Plant parts = Partes de la planta)
Parallel title: Partes de la planta
In English and Spanish.
 Includes index.
 ISBN 978-1-5081-4742-8 (library binding)
 1. Roots (Botany)—Juvenile literature. 2. Plants—Juvenile literature. I. Title.
 QK644.B564 2016
 575.5'4—dc23

Manufactured in the United States of America

CPSIA Compliance Information: Batch #BW16PK: For Further Information contact Rosen Publishing, New York, New York at 1-800-237-9932

Contenido / Contents

Partes escondidas	4
Bien plantada	8
A tomar el agua	12
Los nutrientes son importantes	15
Dos tipos de raíces	16
Comer la raíz	20
Palabras que debes aprender	24
Índice	24
Sitios de Internet	24

Hidden Parts	4
Firmly Planted	8
Taking In Water	12
Nutrients Are Important	15
Two Kinds of Roots	16
Eating Roots	20
Words to Know	24
Index	24
Websites	24

No siempre puedes ver
todas las partes de una planta.
¡Las raíces casi siempre
están escondidas!

You can't always see every
part of a plant. Roots are
almost always hidden!

Las raíces crecen bajo tierra. Tienen funciones muy importantes.

Roots grow under the ground. They have many important jobs.

Las raíces sujetan la planta
al suelo, para que el viento no
se la lleve por el aire o la tumbe.

Roots keep a plant in the
ground. It won't blow away
or tip over.

10

Las raíces ayudan a la planta a estar derecha.

Roots help a plant stand up straight.

Las raíces absorben el agua del suelo. Las plantas necesitan agua para crecer.

Roots take in water from the dirt. Plants need water to grow.

Las raíces también absorben nutrientes. Los nutrientes son pedacitos diminutos de materia. Las plantas los necesitan para crecer.

Roots also take in nutrients. Nutrients are tiny pieces of matter. Plants need them to grow, too.

Hay dos tipos de raíces.
La **raíz primaria** es larga y
gruesa. Apunta hacia abajo.

There are two kinds of roots.
A **taproot** is long and thick.
It points down.

17

Las **raíces fibrosas** tienen muchas raíces pequeñas. Se extienden por toda la tierra.

Fibrous roots have many small roots. They grow throughout the dirt.

Muchas plantas tienen raíces que podemos comer. ¿Sabías que las zanahorias y las remolachas son raíces?

Many plants have roots we can eat. Did you know carrots and beets are roots?

21

La próxima vez que salgas, fíjate en la tierra. ¿Hay raíces allá abajo?

The next time you go outside, look at the ground. Are there roots under there?

PALABRAS QUE DEBES APRENDER / WORDS TO KNOW

(la) raíz fibrosa /
fibrous root

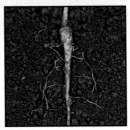

(la) raíz primaria /
taproot

ÍNDICE / INDEX

A
agua / water, 12

N
nutrientes / nutrients, 15

R
raíces fibrosas / fibrous
    roots, 19
raíz primaria / taproot, 16

SITIOS DE INTERNET / WEBSITES

Due to the changing nature of Internet links, PowerKids Press has developed an online list of websites related to the subject of this book. This site is updated regularly. Please use this link to access the list: www.powerkidslinks.com/part/root